MW00912516

SNAP™ CUBE CHALLENGES

BOOK 1

Robert Burton

Cuisenaire® Company of America, Inc.

Dedication

To Rena B. and Wendy J. and all of those beautiful people that comprise that very Special population.
I gratefully acknowledge Debbie and Abe for their love, support, and gift of humor.

Executive Editor: Doris Hirschhorn
Project Editor: ToniAnn Guadagnoli

Production/Manufacturing Director: Janet Yearian
Production/Manufacturing Manager: Karen Edmonds
Production/Manufacturing Coordinator: Mark Pierce

Design Director: Phyllis Aycock
Cover and Interior Designer: Tracey Munz
Composition and Line Art: Cathy Pawlowski

Copyright ©2000 Cuisenaire® Company of America, Inc. All rights reserved.

This book is published by Cuisenaire® Company of America,
an imprint of Pearson Education.

Cuisenaire® Company of America, Inc.
299 Jefferson Road
Parsippany, NJ 07054-0480
Customer Service: 800-237-3142

Limited reproduction permission: The publisher grants permission to individual teachers who have purchased this book to reproduce the blackline masters as needed for use with their own students. Reproduction for an entire school or school district or for commercial use is prohibited.

The word CUISENAIRE and the color sequence of the rods, cubes, and squares are trademarks of Cuisenaire® Company of America, Inc., registered in the United States and other countries.

Printed in the United States of America.
Order Number 030515
ISBN 1-57452-151-9

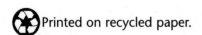Printed on recycled paper.

1 2 3 4 5 6 7 –ML– 02 01 00 99

Table of Contents

Introduction

What are Snap™ Cubes?

Snap Cubes are $\frac{3}{4}$-inch interlocking cubes that come in 10 colors and connect on all six sides. Snap™ Cubes help students understand the mathematical ideas connected to number, measurement, and geometry. They are ideal for exploring patterns and increasing spatial reasoning skills.

What is a Snap Cube Challenge?

A Snap Cube Challenge is an activity that gives children the opportunity to build three-dimensional structures from two-dimensional drawings. As children experiment with different combinations of Snap Cubes, they improve their visual perception and their spatial sense. The Challenges have been placed in order of difficulty. As children move through the activities, the cube manipulation and resulting formations will be increasingly more complex.

How do I start?

Before attempting the Challenges, give students time for play and free exploration. Distribute 20 to 25 Snap Cubes to each student. Tell the class they are to experiment with the cubes. Suggest that they work with a partner to build different shapes and then compare them. After 20 to 30 minutes, invite students to talk about the shapes they built and to discuss what they notice about the cubes.

How should I use this in my classroom?

You can use Snap Cube Challenges in a variety of ways—as whole-class lessons, as individual assignments, or at a learning center—throughout the school year. Include a Challenge as an opening activity for a geometry unit, use one when teaching two-dimensional versus three-dimensional thinking, or make several available as choice activities during math time.

The pages are designed with wide margins and perforations to allow flexibility. For example, you can remove a page and either laminate it or put it in a plastic sleeve. You might prefer to three-hole punch the pages and place them in a binder so that you can make copies for student handouts. Still another option is to simply copy a particular challenge onto clear acetate and then display it on the overhead projector.

Each activity contains one or more questions that encourage student to reflect upon their work. They can be used to promote a small-group or whole-class discussion. Sometimes you might ask a student to give a written response. Other times, you may choose to omit the questions.

About the Multiforms

All the Challenges begin with two or more Multiforms. A Multiform is a particular combination of Snap™ Cubes (see page 7) that children must build to solve each Challenge. There are seven different Multiforms used for the activities in this book.

The prong of the Snap Cube may pose some difficulty when students try to create forms to look like those pictured. Since the prongs are not featured in the illustrations, instruct students to ignore the extra prongs that may "stick out" on their forms. For an added challenge, you might suggest that they manipulate the cubes so that there are no visible prongs.

Recording

Recording is optional. Decide whether recording is appropriate for your students. If it is, point out that each Multiform has an identity, a specific letter associated with it. It would be best if page 7 is easily accessible to students so that they may refer to the Multiform identities (letters). Have students write in the letter of the corresponding Multiform to show where each form fits in the structure as shown below.

Several of the Challenges can be built using a number of different combinations. The simpler the Challenge, the more likely it will have multiple solutions. When more than one solution is called for, the structure is pictured several times. Students can record their solutions in any order as shown below.

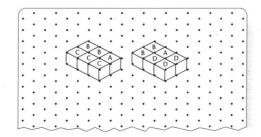

In Section 3, Clones, students work with two identical sets of Multiforms. The recording may be a bit more difficult. In this section, students label their sets as 1 and 2. So there will be an A and an A2, a B and a B2, and so on. The following solution is an example of such a situation.

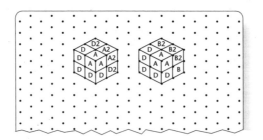

Isometric dot paper and Snap™ Cube grid paper are provided as alternatives to the recording sheets. Students may use the grid paper to keep a top-view record of the forms that did or did not work. Students may use the dot paper to draw each solution rather than just labeling the forms. This is a challenging recording system, providing practice in visualizing graphic representations and drawing three-dimensional objects in two dimensions.

Author's Note

The most important components to the success of this series are a desire to learn, think, and apply. These Challenges provide an avenue for developing mathematical confidence in a nonroutine manner. Some exercises may be more challenging than others. Encourage students to experiment, even if they make mistakes. As children experiment, these activities can produce an "I can do it" attitude. By giving children the necessary encouragement, you will ultimately produce the smiles that come from success.

SECTION 1
Multiforms—
A Place to Start

A form is one or more Snap™ Cubes snapped together.

Build the forms shown below. For any one form, use the same color of cubes.

This set of forms is called the Snap Cube Multiforms.

You will combine these Multiforms to build structures in the activities that follow. The letters can be used to record and identify the different forms.

Form A   Form B   Form C   Form D

Form E   Form F   Form G

© Cuisenaire Company of America, Inc.

Which Three?

Build this structure with three Multiforms.

Which forms did you use?

The letters of the Multiforms can be written in the shapes shown below. (The first one is done for you.)

Now exchange one of the forms for one you did not use.

Build the structure again.

Record your new solution in the remaining shape below.

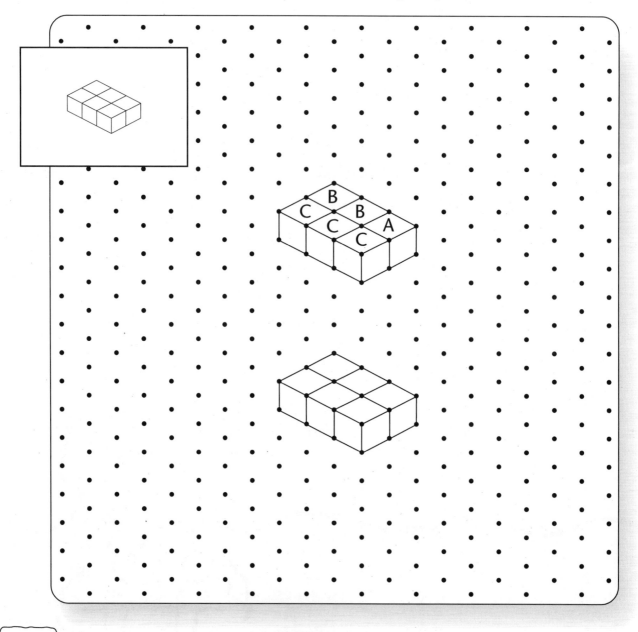

© Cuisenaire Company of America, Inc.

Which Three?

Build this structure with three Multiforms.

This can be done with four different combinations of forms.

Find all the combinations. Each time record the forms you use.

How did you decide which forms to select?

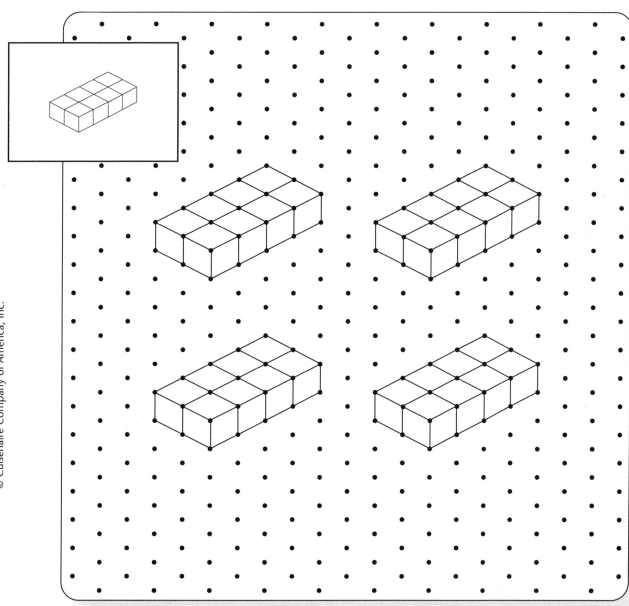

© Cuisenaire Company of America, Inc.

Which Three?

Build this structure with three Multiforms.

This can be done with four different combinations of forms.

Find all the combinations. Each time record the forms you use.

How did you decide which forms to select?

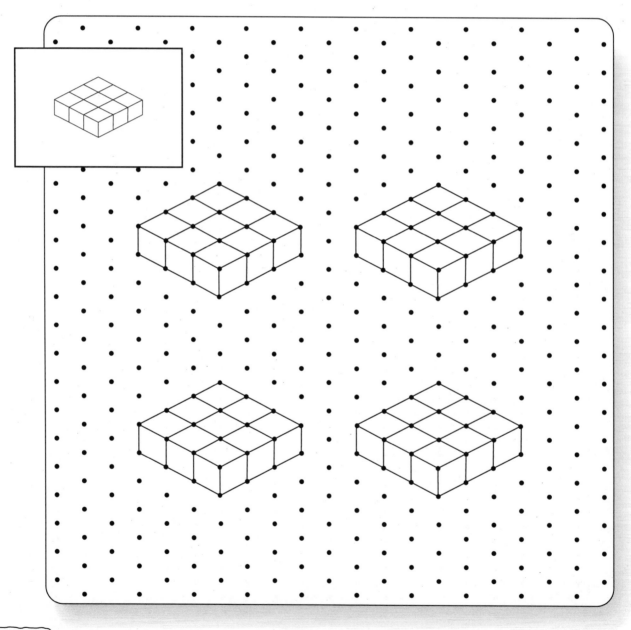

© Cuisenaire Company of America, Inc.

ACTIVITY 4

Which Three?

Build this structure with three Multiforms.

This can be done with three different combinations of forms.

Find all the combinations. Each time record the forms you use.

How did you decide which forms to select?

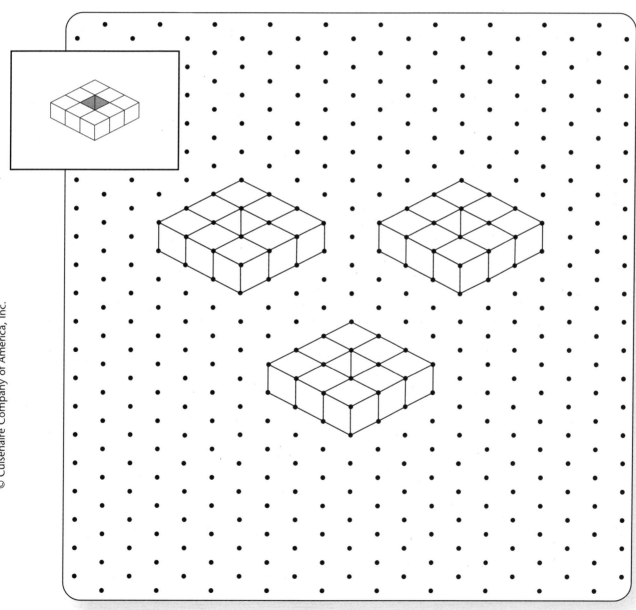

© Cuisenaire Company of America, Inc.

Which Four?

Build this structure with four Multiforms.

This can be done with three different combinations of forms.

Find all the combinations. Each time record the forms you use.

How did you decide which forms to select?

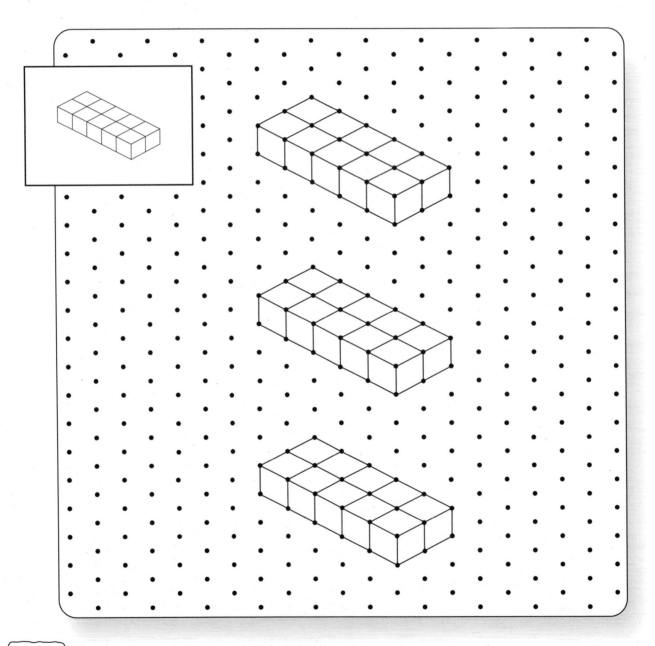

© Cuisenaire Company of America, Inc.

SNAP™ CUBE CHALLENGES · Book 1

Which Five?

Build this structure with five Multiforms.

This can be done with three different combinations of forms.

Find all the combinations. Each time record the forms you use.

How did you decide which forms to select?

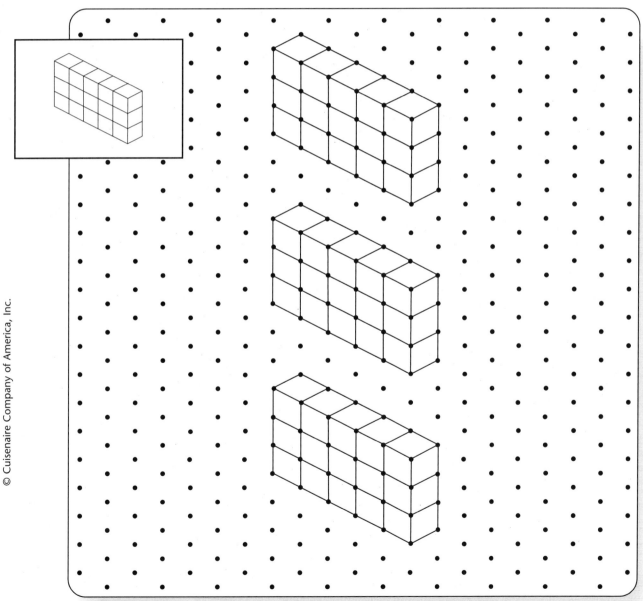

© Cuisenaire Company of America, Inc.

Which Five?

Build this structure with five Multiforms.

Record the forms you use.

How did you decide which forms to select?
Can the structure be made with another
combination of forms?

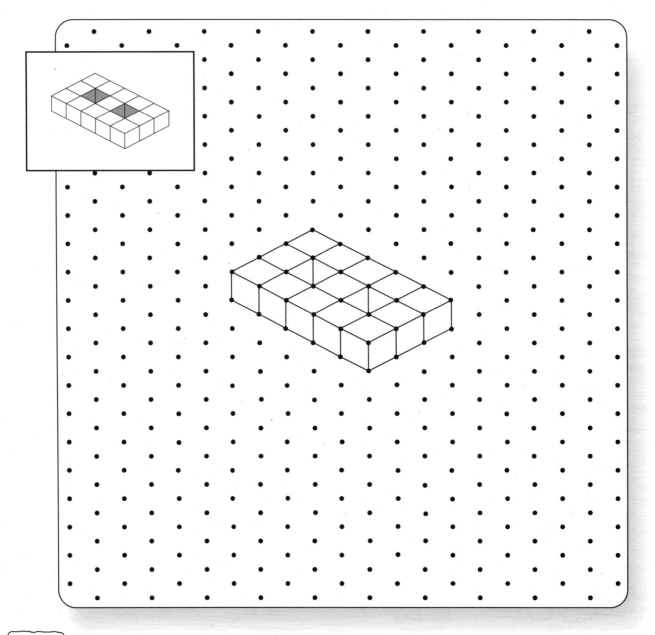

© Cuisenaire Company of America, Inc.

Which Six?

Build this structure with six Multiforms.

This can be done with two different combinations of forms.

Find all the combinations. Each time record the forms you use.

How did you decide which one of the seven Multiforms to leave out?

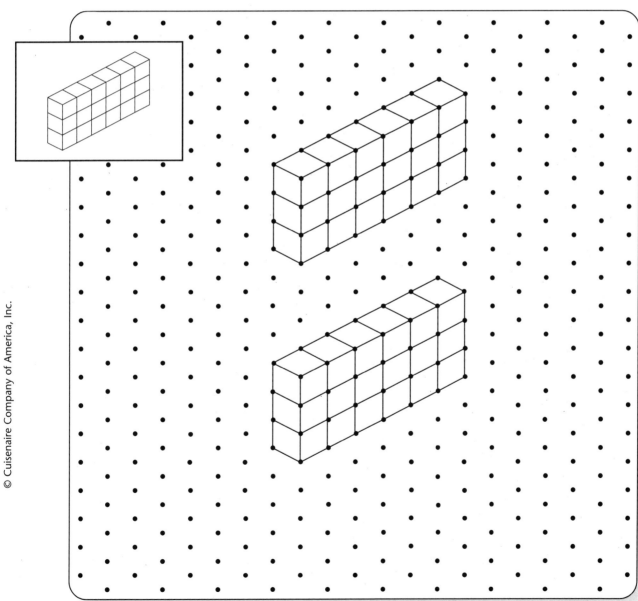

© Cuisenaire Company of America, Inc.

Using All Seven

Build this structure using all seven Multiforms.

Record your arrangement.

Find and record another arrangement of the seven forms.

What was your thinking as you searched for the solution?

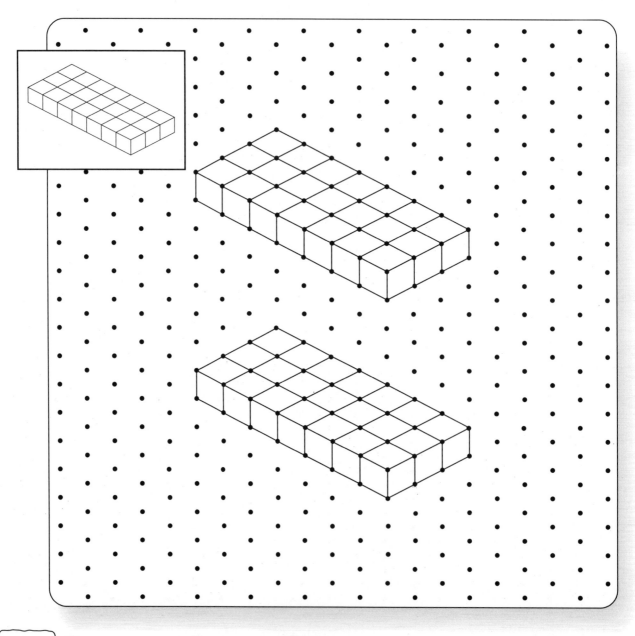

© Cuisenaire Company of America, Inc.

Using All Seven

Build this structure using all seven Multiforms.

Record your arrangement.

Find and record another arrangement of the seven forms.

Suppose you had another set of Multiforms.
Which form would fill the space?

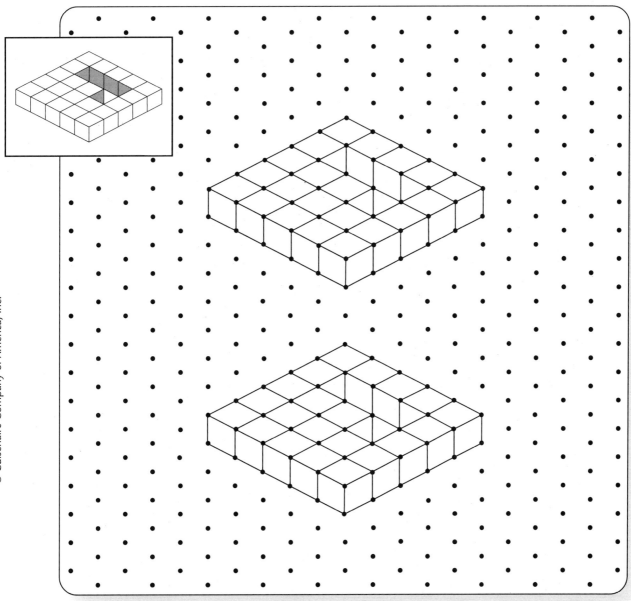

© Cuisenaire Company of America, Inc.

Using All Seven

Build this structure using all seven Multiforms.

Record your arrangement.

Find and record another arrangement of the seven forms.

Suppose you had another set of Multiforms.
Which two forms would fill the space?

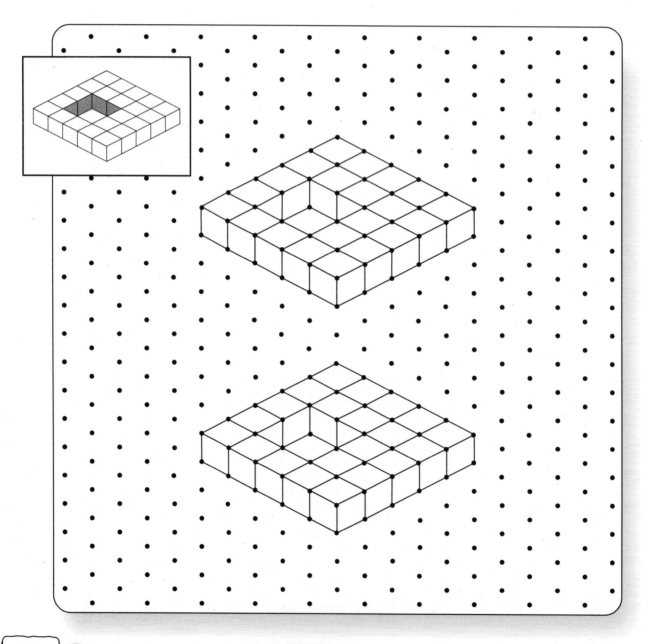

© Cuisenaire Company of America, Inc.

SECTION 2
Silhouettes

In the first section, students built only flat rectangular structures, some solid, some with holes. In this section, students are invited to build structures that are not square or rectangular. Although flat, these irregular structures, referred to as Silhouettes, usually have several protruding cubes. Because the Multiforms do not always "fit" together as "neatly" as they do when made into rectangles and squares, Silhouettes can be more challenging.

Many of the Silhouettes have a geometric balance, offering an excellent opportunity to talk about symmetry. Introduce the "mirror line" or line of symmetry—the line that divides the structure into two identical parts. Being able to identify the line of symmetry can make solving each Challenge easier.

© Cuisenaire Company of America, Inc.

Which Two?

Build this structure with two Multiforms.

This can be done with two different combinations of forms.

Find both combinations. Each time record the forms you use.

What was your thinking as you searched for the solutions?

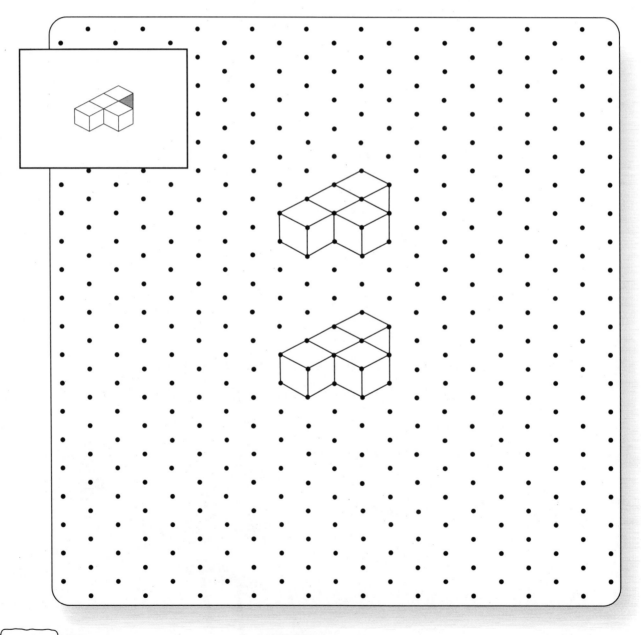

© Cuisenaire Company of America, Inc.

Which Three?

Build this structure with three Multiforms.

This can be done with two different combinations of forms.

Find both combinations. Each time record the forms you use.

What was your thinking as you searched for the solutions?

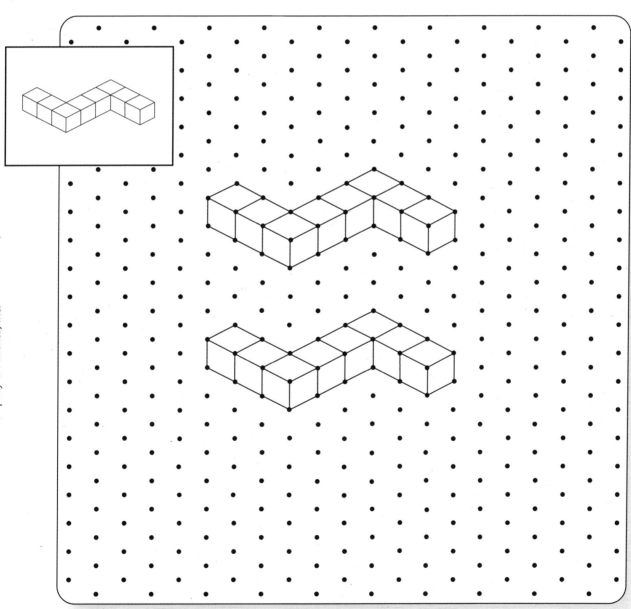

© Cuisenaire Company of America, Inc.

Which Three?

Build this structure with three Multiforms.

This can be done with two different combinations of forms.

Find both combinations. Each time record the forms you use.

You can also build this structure with only two forms.
Can you find them?
Can you find a different pair?

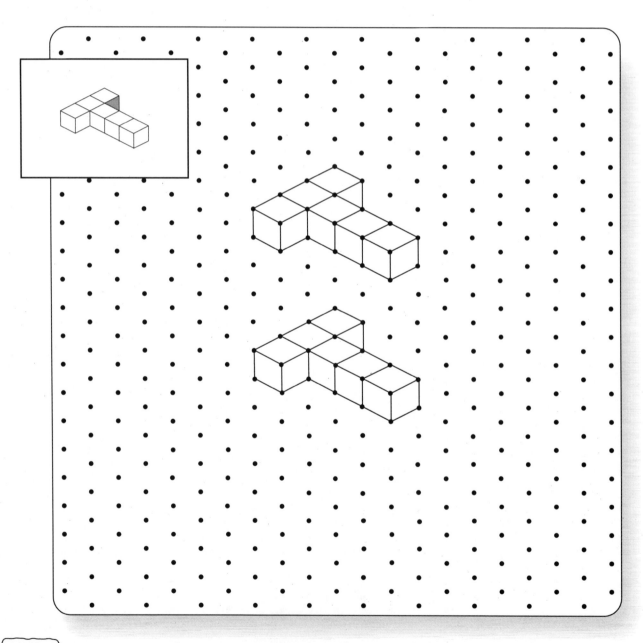

© Cuisenaire Company of America, Inc.

Three Ways

Build this structure with three Multiforms.

This can be done with three different combinations of forms.

Find all the combinations. Each time record the forms you use.

What was your thinking as you searched for the solutions?

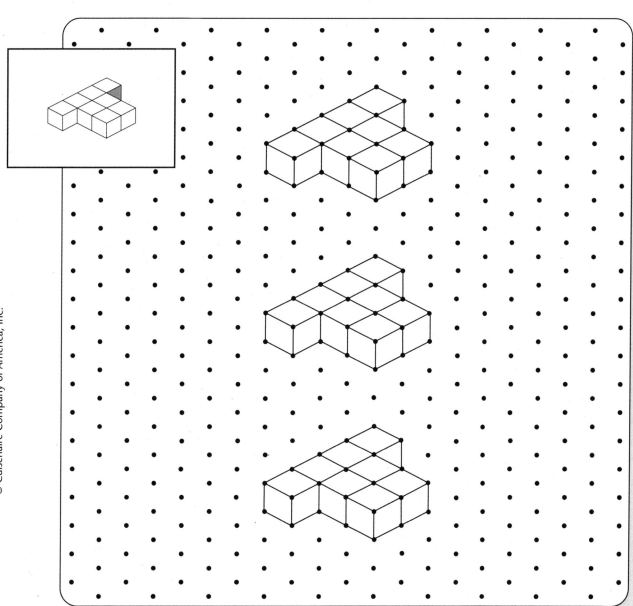

© Cuisenaire Company of America, Inc.

Seven Ways

Build this structure with three Multiforms. This can be done with two different combinations of forms. Each time record the forms you use.

Then build this structure with four forms. This can be done with five different combinations of forms. Each time record the forms you use.

What was your thinking as you searched for the solutions?

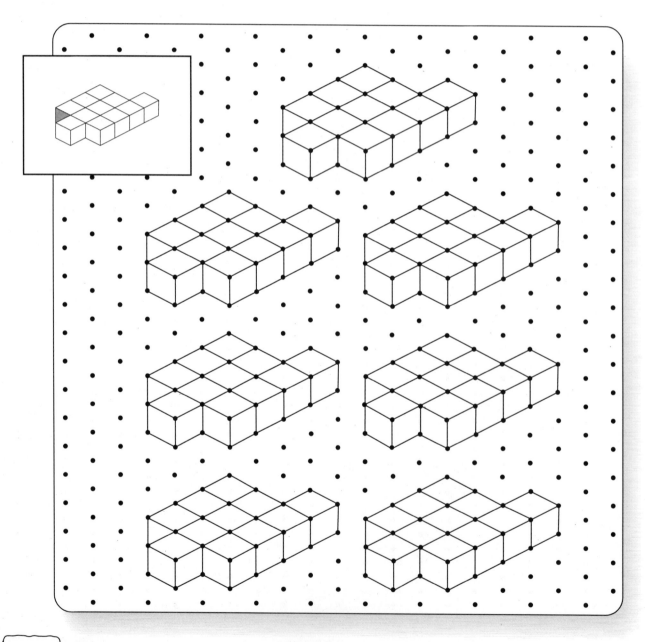

© Cuisenaire Company of America, Inc.

Select the Multiforms you think you need to build this structure.

Now try to build the structure.

Try other forms if your prediction does not work.

Which forms worked?
Why did you predict what you predicted?
What was your thinking as you searched for the solutions?

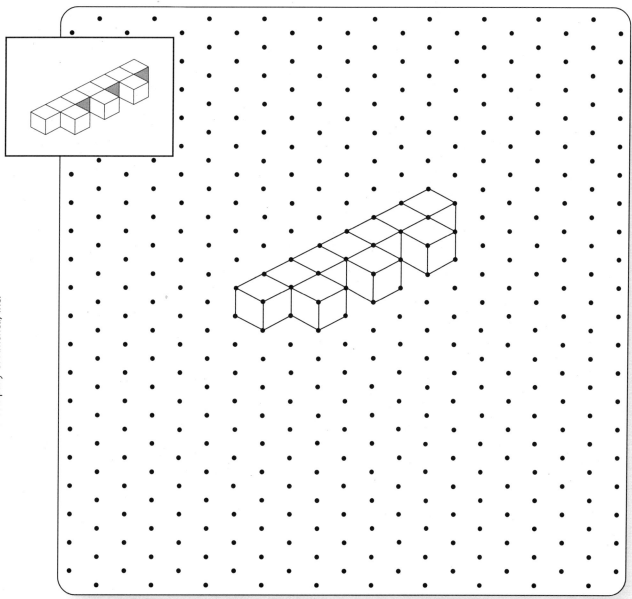

© Cuisenaire Company of America, Inc.

Which Forms?

Select the Multiforms you think you need to build this structure.

Now try to build the structure.

Try other forms if your prediction does not work.

This can be done with at least three different combinations.

Which forms worked?
Why did you predict what you predicted?
What was your thinking as you searched for the solutions?

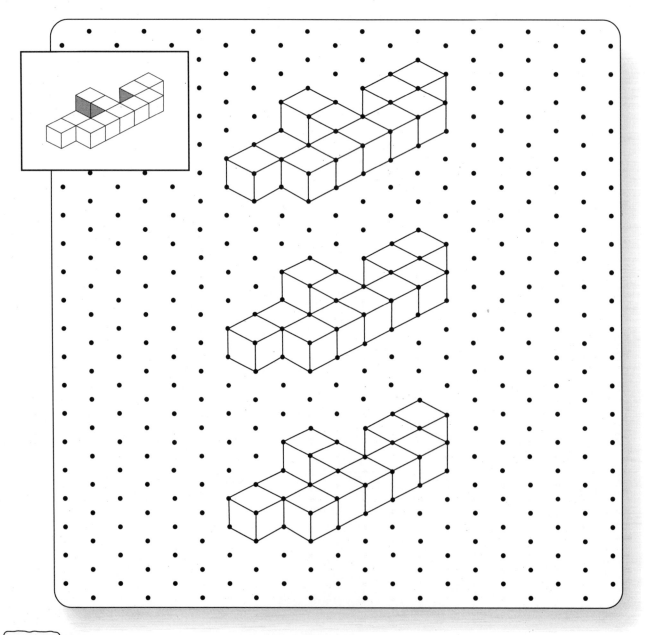

© Cuisenaire Company of America, Inc.

Select the Multiforms you think you need to build this structure.

Now try to build the structure.

Try other forms if your prediction does not work.

This can be done with at least two different combinations.

Which forms worked?
Why did you predict what you predicted?
What was your thinking as you searched for the solutions?

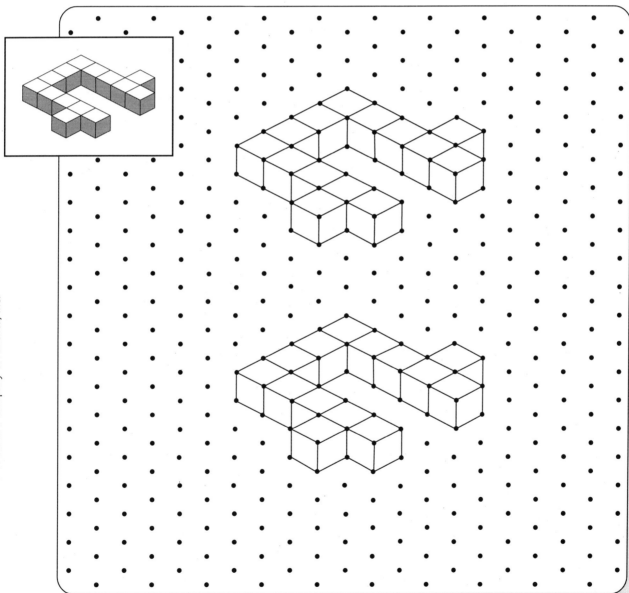

© Cuisenaire Company of America, Inc.

Which Forms?

Select the Multiforms you think you need to build this structure.

Now try to build the structure.

Try other forms if your prediction does not work.

What was your thinking as you searched for the solution?

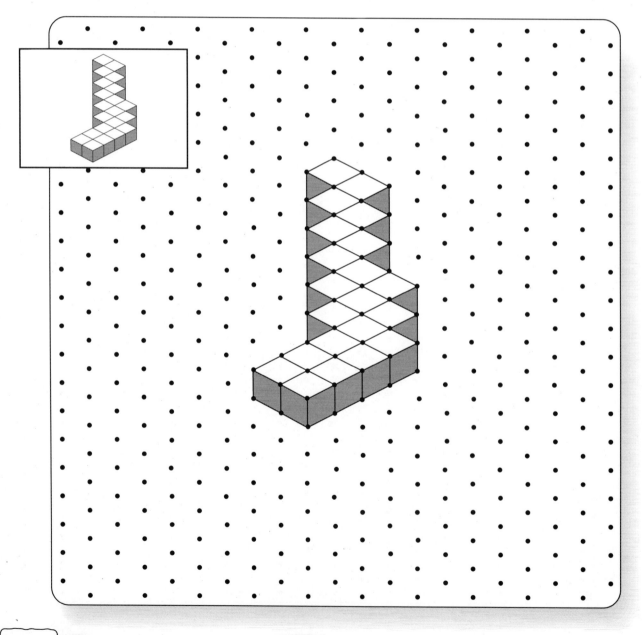

© Cuisenaire Company of America, Inc.

SECTION 3
Clones

This section is the most difficult since the Challenges require two identical sets of Multiforms, thus the name, Clones. In addition, the structures that are to be built are multilayered. That is, when a structure is placed on a table, at least one Snap™ Cube will not touch the tabletop, no matter which way the structure is positioned.

The formations in Activities 21 through 24 are rectangle in shape, whereas those in Activities 25 through 29 are <u>almost</u> rectangular. The shape of these structures provides an opportunity to talk about length, width, height, and volume. With experience, students can see that computing the product of the dimensions (length × width × height) is a good strategy for judging how many Snap Cubes are needed to build the structure.

© Cuisenaire Company of America, Inc.

Building Boxes

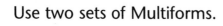

Use two sets of Multiforms.

Build this box using Form B and two of Form D.

Now try to use four Multiforms. This can be done with at least two different combinations of forms.

Record your solutions.

Why is it impossible to build this box without using Forms A, B, or D?

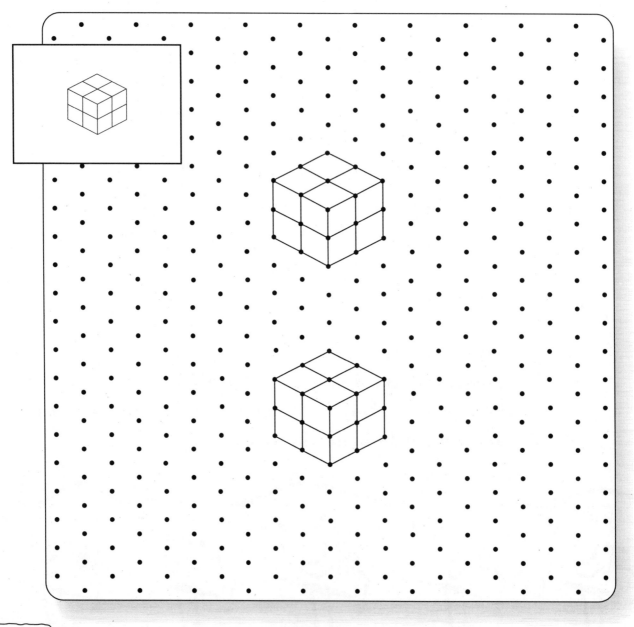

© Cuisenaire Company of America, Inc.

Building Boxes

Use two sets of Multiforms.

Build this box with four forms.

This can be done with at least seven different combinations of forms.

Find as many as you can.

Record your solutions.

How did you find the solutions?

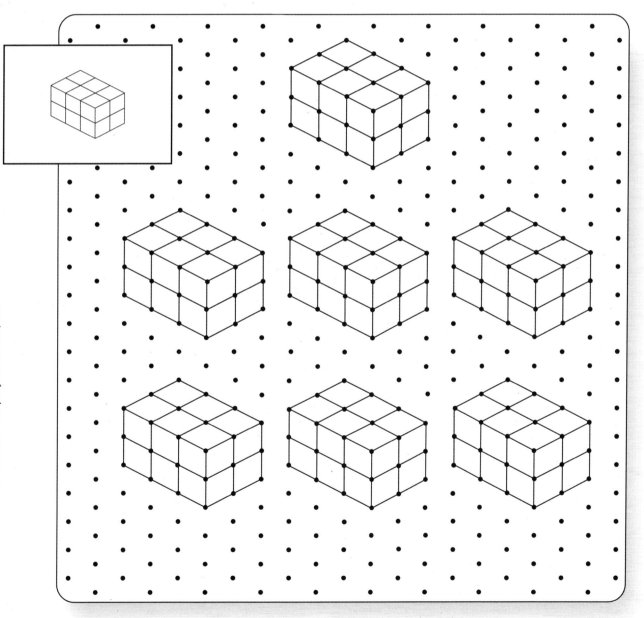

© Cuisenaire Company of America, Inc.

Building Boxes

Use two sets of Multiforms.

Build this box with five forms.

This can be done with at least six different combinations of forms.

Find as many as you can.

Record your solutions.

How did you find the solutions?

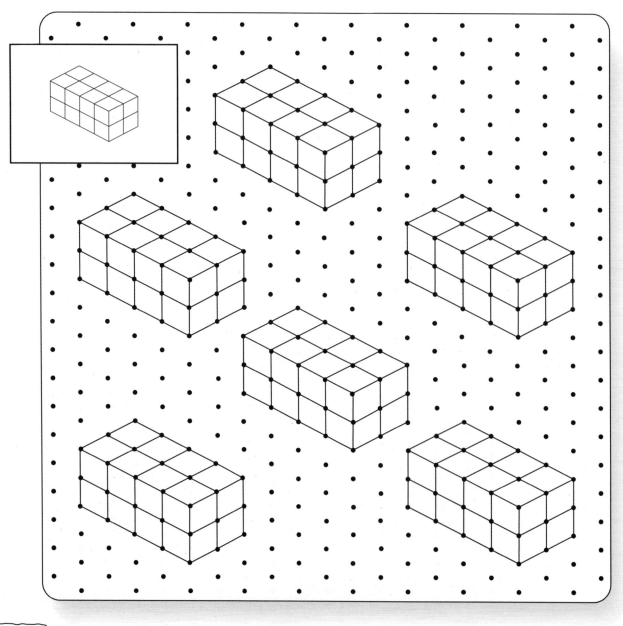

© Cuisenaire Company of America, Inc.

Building Boxes

Use two sets of Multiforms.

Build this box with six forms.

This can be done with at least six different combinations of forms.

Find as many as you can.

Record your solutions.

How did you find the solutions?

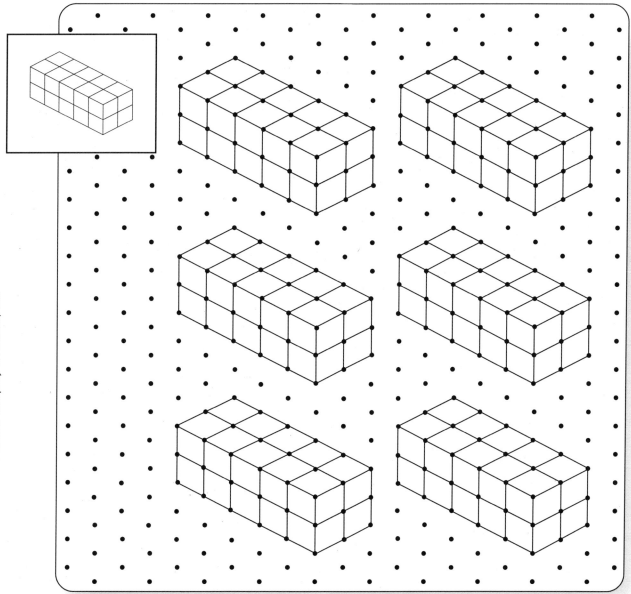

© Cuisenaire Company of America, Inc.

Building Shelves

Use two sets of Multiforms.

Build this shelf with four forms.

This can be done with at least three different combinations of forms.

Find as many as you can.

Record your solutions.

How did you decide which forms to select?

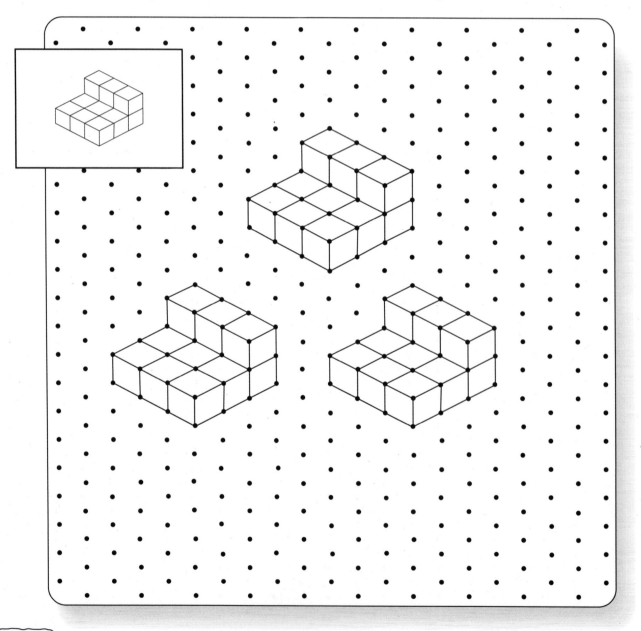

© Cuisenaire Company of America, Inc.

Building Shelves

Use two sets of Multiforms.

Build this shelf with six forms.

Record your solution.

How did you decide which forms to select?

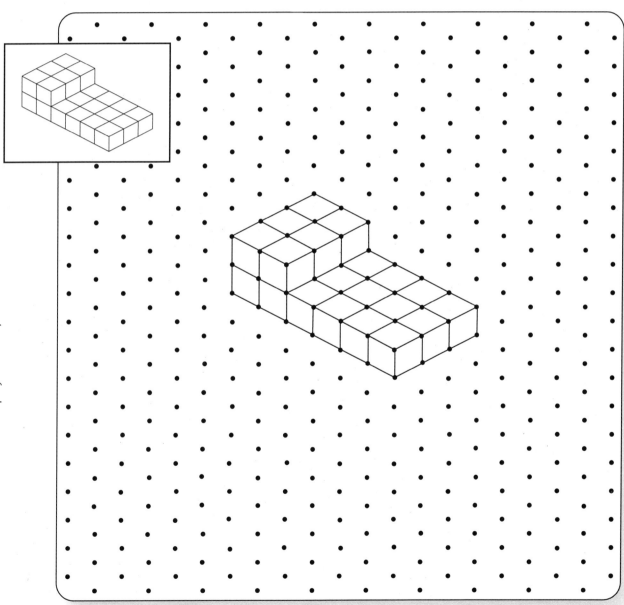

© Cuisenaire Company of America, Inc.

Building Shelves

Use two sets of Multiforms.

Build this shelf with eight forms.

Record your solution.

How did you decide which forms to select?

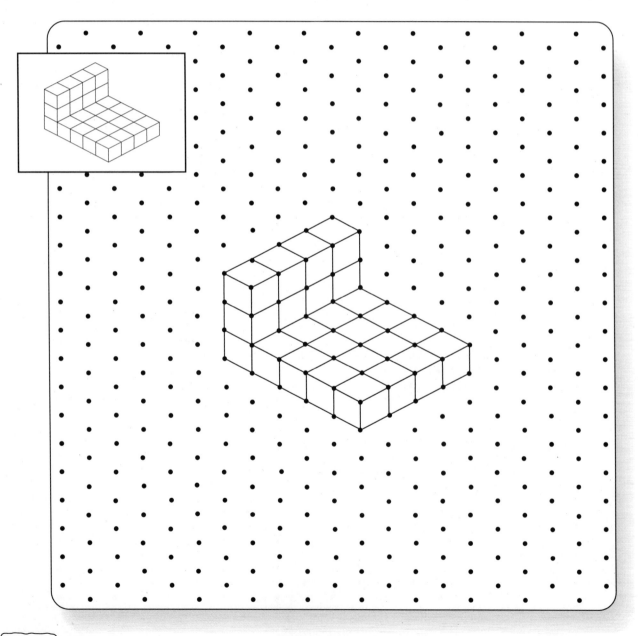

SNAP™ CUBE CHALLENGES · Book 1

© Cuisenaire Company of America, Inc.

Building Shelves

Use two sets of Multiforms.

Build this shelf with eight forms.

Record your solution.

How did you decide which forms to select?

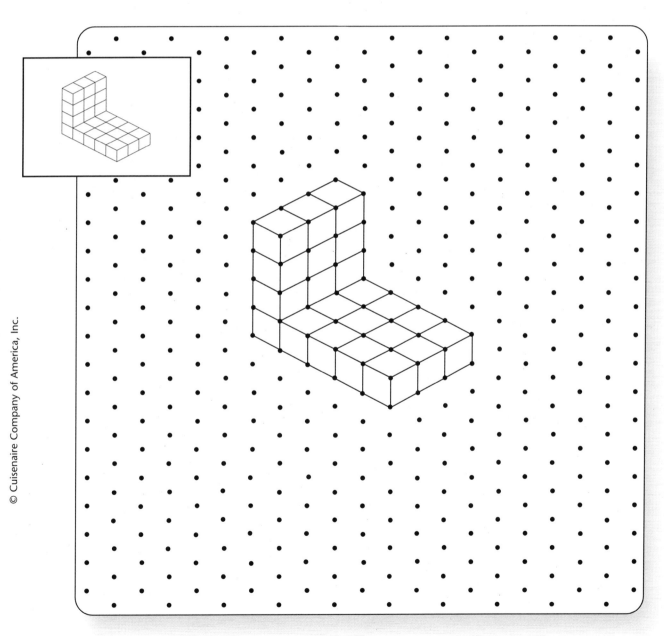

© Cuisenaire Company of America, Inc.

ACTIVITY 29 — Building Shelves

Use two sets of Multiforms.

Build this shelf with 13 forms.

Record your solution.

How did you decide which forms to select?

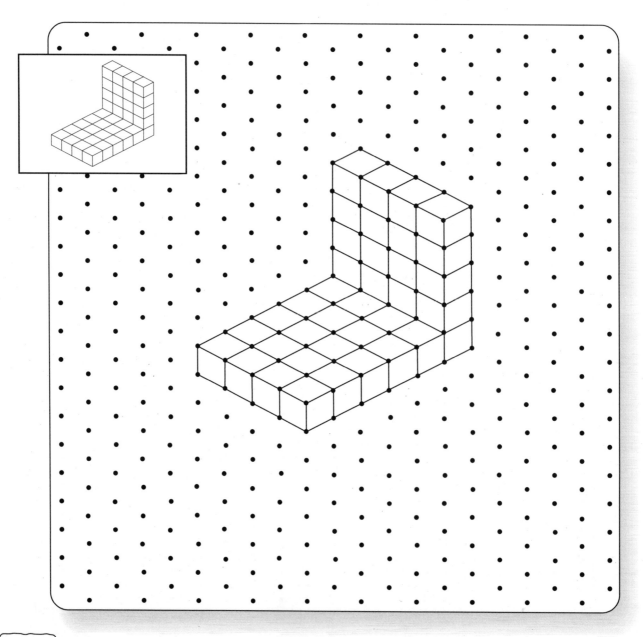

© Cuisenaire Company of America, Inc.

Use two sets of Multiforms.

Build this shelf with the entire set of 14 forms!

How did you find the solution?

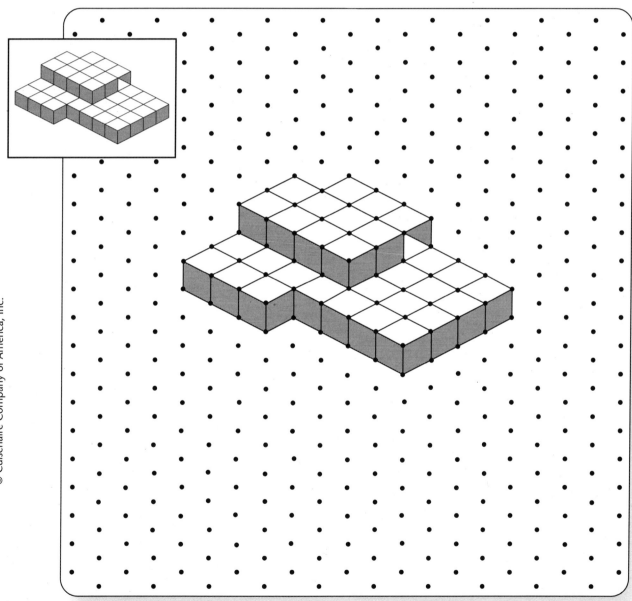

© Cuisenaire Company of America, Inc.

SECTION 4
Solutions and Recording Paper

In this section are solutions and typical responses to each Challenge. Each solution is recorded with the letter identities of the Multiforms as explained in the Introduction.

Also included are blackline masters of Isometric Dot Paper and Snap™ Cube Grid Paper. Instead of using the preprinted format that appears on every activity, children can make their own drawings. With the Isometric Dot Paper, students can show three-dimensionality. With the Snap Cube Grid Paper, students can record each face of the structure.

Encourage students to find as many solutions as they can. Urge them not to limit themselves to the number of diagrams shown. It is very possible that there are still solutions to be uncovered!

© Cuisenaire Company of America, Inc.

Solutions

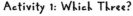

Activity 1: Which Three?
Two combinations:

Activity 2: Which Three?
Four combinations:

Answers will vary. Some possible responses:

- I just kept trying different forms.
- I started with Form F and saw that if I added Form A to the three cubes, I would have more than half of what I needed. Then I added Form C to complete the structure.

Activity 3: Which Three?
Four combinations:

Answers will vary. Some possible responses:

- If I had two Form Ds it would have worked.
- I tried the other forms but a cube was always sticking out or there was a hole.

Activity 4: Which Three?
Three combinations:

Answers will vary. Some possible responses:

- I eliminated Forms E and G immediately because they would make it impossible to leave the center empty.
- I found the combination of Forms A, D, and F. Then noticed that Forms B and C could be arranged to look like Forms A and F.

Activity 5: Which Four?
Three combinations:

Answers will vary. A possible response:

There was no way to get two straight lines with five cubes in each line with the other form.

Activity 6: Which Five?
Three combinations:

Answers will vary. A possible response:

I took Forms A, D, E, and F and made a rectangle. Then I needed one more row of three cubes. So I used Form C and added an extra row to the rectangle.

Activity 7: Which Five?
One combination:

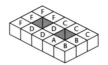

Answers will vary. A possible response:

Again I eliminated Form G because the centers needed to be empty. I was able to make the shape with four forms—B, C, E, and F, but then realized I was supposed to use five forms. I decided to take out Form E and I replaced it with Forms D and A.

Solutions

Activity 8: Which Six?
Two combinations:

Answers will vary. A possible response:

I made two squares the same size. Each square used three forms. Forms A, F, and G made one square. Forms B, D, and E made the other square.

Activity 9: Using All Seven
Two combinations:

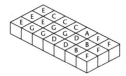 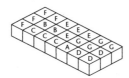

Answers will vary. A possible response:

I made a 3 × 5 structure with Forms D, E, F, G, then added Form C. That only used five forms, so I put Forms A and B together and took away Form C.

Activity 10: Using All Seven
Two combinations:

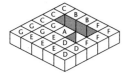 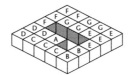

Form F would fill the missing space.

Activity 11: Using All Seven
Two combinations:

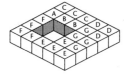 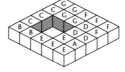

Forms A and D would fill the missing space.

Activity 12: Which Two?
Two combinations:

Answers will vary. Some possible responses:

- The structure looked just like Form E.
- I saw two rows. One had three cubes and the other had one cube.

Activity 13: Which Three?
Two combinations:

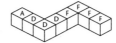 

Answers will vary. A possible response:

I counted the cubes in parts. I saw four cubes like in Form F, then one cube (Form A), and then three cubes (Form C).

Activity 14: Which Three?
Two combinations:

This can also be built with Forms B and E or Forms F and A.

Activity 15: Three Ways
Three combinations:

Answers will vary. A possible response:

The structure looked just like two Form Fs—back-to-back. So I used Form F on one side and then Form C and Form A to make another Form F on the other side.

Solutions

Activity 16: Seven Ways
Seven combinations:

Answers will vary. A possible response:

I looked at the shape and saw that the bottom could be Form E. So I used it for the bottom and Form F for the top and put Form C between them.

Activity 17: Which Forms?
One combination:

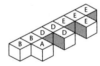

Answers will vary. A possible response:

I looked at the drawing and started at the right. I saw Form E, then Form D, and then Form D again. I did not have two Form Ds, so I made the same shape from Forms A and B.

Activity 18: Which Forms?
Three combinations:

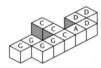

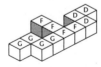 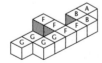

Answers will vary. A possible response:

I saw the structure and split it down the middle. I used Form C as a divider. Then I needed two of Form Gs (one for each side of Form C). I had to use Forms D and A on the right side of Form C to make the same shape as Form G on the left.

Activity 19: Which Forms?
Two combinations:

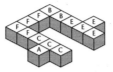 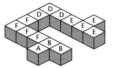

Answers will vary. A possible response:

I built one side, then matched the other side to it.

Activity 20: Which Forms?
One combination:

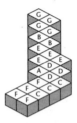

Answers will vary. A possible response:

I saw that the top was made of zig-zags so I started with Form G. Then I added Forms B and E because they fit the spaces which would hold two and three cubes diagonally. After that, I used Forms F and C to fill up the bottom and Forms D and A to put the top and bottom together.

Activity 21: Building Boxes
Two combinations:

A, A2, D, D2   *A, B, B2, D*

Answers will vary. A possible response:

All the other forms have at least one dimension that is more than two cubes.

Solutions

Activity 22: Building Boxes
Seven combinations:

B, B2, E, E2   *B, B2, F, F2*

B, B2, G, G2   *B, C, C2, F*

B, D, D2, E   *B, D, D2, G*   *C, C2, D, D2*

Answers will vary. Some possible responses:

- I started with a 2 × 2 × 2 structure made of Forms B and two Ds. I added a square made of one Form B and two Form As.
- I built a larger structure using two Form Bs and two Form Fs, then repeated it.

Activity 23: Building Boxes
Six combinations:

B, B2, F, F2, G   *B, C, C2, F, F2*

B, D, D2, E, E2   *B, D, D2, E, G*

B, D, D2, F, F2   *B, D, D2, G, G2*

Answers will vary. Some possible responses:
- I built a partial layer, then duplicated it, and put in Form B.
- I built a 3 × 2 × 2 cube, then added a flat 2 × 2 square.

Activity 24: Building Boxes
Six combinations:

B, B2, F, F2, G, G2   *B, C, D, F, F2, G*

B, D, D2, F, F2, G   *C, C2, D, D2, E, E2*

C, C2, D, D2, F, F2   *B, C, D, D2, F, G*

Answers will vary. Some possible responses:

- I put two Form Es together into a 5 × 2 flat rectangle leaving two corners missing. I covered up the middle with two Form Bs and saw that I could use two Form Ds for the corners.
- I made a 2 × 5 flat rectangle with two Form Fs and one Form B. I put two Form Bs together on the top. I kept looking until I realized Form D would hook over if I removed one Form B. Then I had six forms.

Activity 25: Building Shelves
Three combinations:

A, D, E, E2

B, D, D2, F   *B, D, D2, G*

Answers will vary.

Solutions

Activity 26: Building Shelves
One combination:

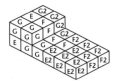

E, E2, F, F2, G, G2

Answers will vary.

Activity 27: Building Shelves
One combination:

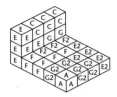

A, C, E, E2, F, F2, G, G2

Answers will vary.

Activity 28: Building Shelves
One combination:

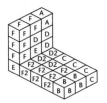

A, B, C, D, D2, E, F, F2

Answers will vary.

Activity 29: Building Shelves
One combination:

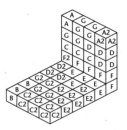

A, A2, B, C, C2, D, D2, E, E2, F, F2, G, G2

Answers will vary.

Activity 30: The Final Challenge
One combination:

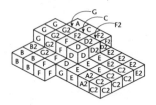

All Forms (A–G and A2–G2)

Answers will vary.

© Cuisenaire Company of America, Inc.

Isometric Dot Paper

© Cuisenaire Company of America, Inc.

Snap™ Cube Grid Paper

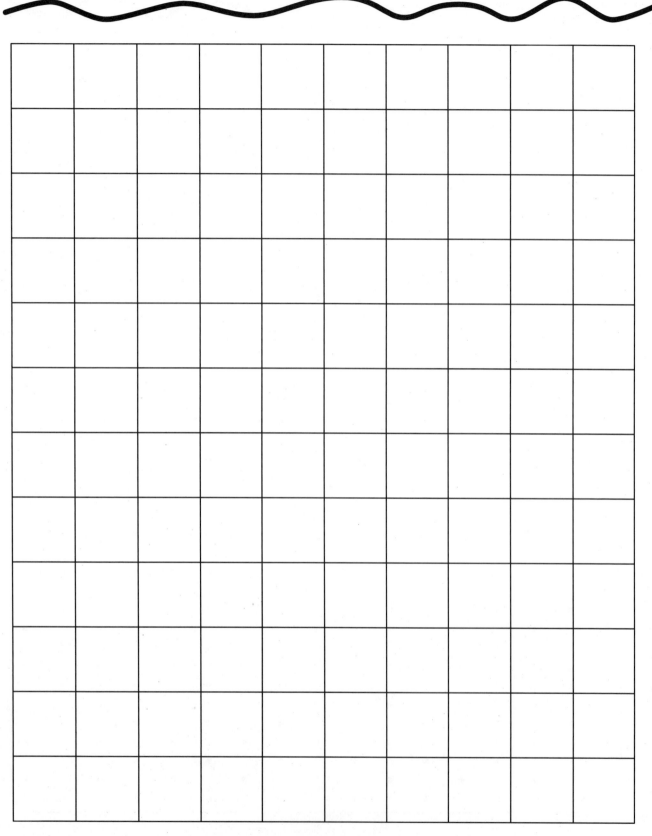

© Cuisenaire Company of America, Inc.